Can You See the Chalkboard?

Dr. Alvin Silverstein,

Virginia Silverstein, and

Laura Silverstein Nunn

My Health

Franklin Watts

A Division of Grolier Publishing

New York • London • Hong Kong • Sydney

Danbury, Connecticut

Photographs ©: Custom Medical Stock Photo: 19, 20, 22 (Teri J. McDermott), 11 (SPL), 26; Nance S. Trueworthy: 18; Photo Researchers: 33 (Mark Clarke/SPL), 12 (Ralph C. Eagle Jr. MD), 7 (Adam Hart-Davis/SPL), 23 (Dr. P. Marazzi/SPL), 31 left (Andrew McClenaghan/SPL), 15 (Hans-Ulrich Osterwalder/SPL), 29, 30, 31 right (David Parker/SPL); PhotoEdit: 35 (M. K. Denny), 6, 24 (Michael Newman); Superstock, Inc.: 9; The Image Works: 27 (M. Antman), 14 (John Eastcott/VVA Momatiuk), 4 (Frank Pedrick); Visuals Unlimited: 36 (Cheyenne Rouse).

Cartoons by Rick Stromoski

Visit Franklin Watts on the Internet at:
http://publishing.grolier.com

Library of Congress Cataloging-in-Publication Data

Silverstein, Alvin.
    Can You See the Chalkboard? / by Alvin Silverstein, Virginia Silverstein, and Laura Silverstein Nunn.
        p.   cm.—(My Health)
    Includes bibliographical references and index.
    Summary: Describes the human eye and how it functions, various visual problems and how they are corrected, and how to take care of one's eyes.
        ISBN 0-531-11783-9 (lib. bdg.)   0-531-13969-7 (pbk.)
        1. Vision disorders—Juvenile literature. 2. Vision—Juvenile literature. 3. Eye—Juvenile literature. [1. Eye. 2. Vision. 3. Senses and sensation.]
    I. Silverstein, Virginia B. II. Nunn, Laura Silverstein. III. Title. IV. Series.
    RE52.S56 2001
    617.7—dc21   00-028983

GROLIER
PUBLISHING

Contents

When Things Look Blurry   5

Inside Your Eyes   7

How Your Eyes See   14

What's Wrong with this Picture?   18

Do You Need Glasses?   25

Are Contacts for You?   29

Take Care of Your Eyes   33

Glossary   38

Learning More   42

Index   45

When Things Look Blurry

Do you have trouble seeing the chalkboard clearly in school? Does the print look blurry when you try to read a book? Do you rub your eyes and squint a lot? These are all signs that your eyes aren't working quite right.

Your eyes are remarkable. You use them to see a rainbow of colors and a variety of shapes. You can see in bright sunshine or in almost total darkness.

Your eyes let you see where you are going. They help you look out for cars before crossing the street. They keep you from bumping into furniture or tripping over toys on the floor. Most importantly, your eyes also help you learn about and understand the world.

Did You Know...

Your eyes are your most important sense organ. About 80 percent of the information your body gathers about the world comes through your eyes.

◀ **Can you see the chalkboard in your classroom at school? If not, tell an adult. You may need to see an eye doctor.**

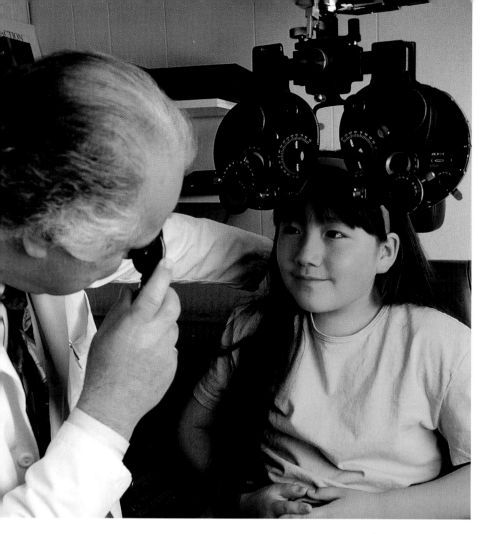

An eye doctor can tell if your eyes are working right.

If you can see objects clearly from both far away and close up, you have good **vision**. But if some things look a little blurry to you, you probably have poor vision. Don't worry, though—an eye doctor can test your eyes to find out what's wrong. You may need eyeglasses to help you see better. Don't worry about that either. If you don't want to wear glasses, you may be able to wear contact lenses instead.

Whether you have perfect vision or wear glasses, there are some things you can do to keep your eyes healthy and strong. Read on to learn more about how your eyes work and what you can do if something goes wrong.

Inside Your Eyes

When you look at yourself in a mirror, you can see only a very small part of your eyes. You see a colored circle with a black dot in the center. That is the front of a large organ called an **eyeball**. An eyeball looks like a big round marble. A marble is hard, but an eyeball is soft. It is filled with a jellylike liquid.

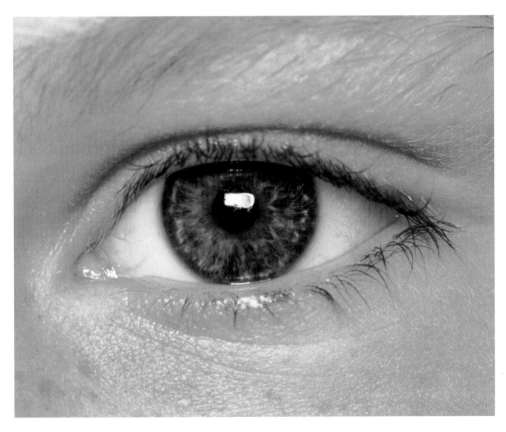

The eyeball is round like a marble, but you see only the front part of it.

Did You Know...

You may not realize it, but your eyes blink all the time. Unless your eyes are closed, you blink between six and thirty times each minute.

Your **eyelids** protect your eyes. You can move them up and down like window shades. You can close them if you see a very bright light or if you want to go to sleep. If an insect or a bit of dust zooms in toward your eyes, your eyelids quickly snap shut—you blink. Blinking is automatic. You don't even have to think about it.

Blinking allows your eyelid to work like a pump. The closing action squeezes out a bit of liquid from your **tear gland** and then spreads it evenly over your **cornea**—the clear covering on the surface of the eye. You make tears all the time. They keep your eyes moist so your cornea won't dry out and get sore.

You can look right through your cornea and see your **iris**—the colored part of the eye. The color of a person's iris depends on the amount of **pigment** in it. Brown eyes have a lot of pigment; blue eyes have less.

The black dot in the middle of your iris is an opening called the **pupil**. Behind the pupil is the **lens**. Light rays enter your eye through the pupil. Muscles inside

8

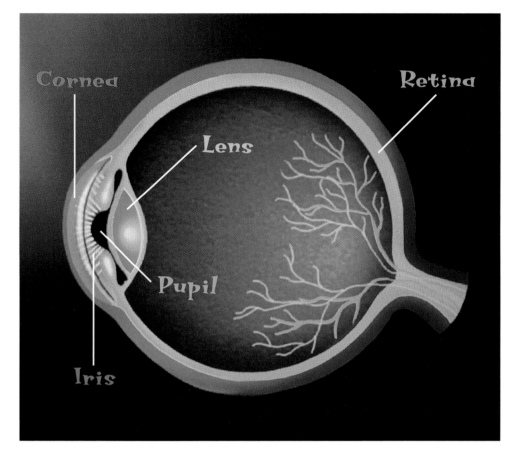

Cornea

Retina

Lens

Pupil

Iris

your iris can change the size of your pupil. When you are in a dark place, your pupil gets large so more light can pass through your lens. When you are in a bright place, your pupil gets small so less light enters your eyeball.

Light rays pass through the liquid in your eyeball and strike the **retina**, a layer of light-sensitive cells that line the back of your eyeball. Here, they form a picture called an **image**. There are two kinds of cells in the retina

Activity 1: How Big Are Your Pupils?

To see how light affects the size of your pupils, stand in front of a mirror in a sunny room. Look closely at your pupils. Cover your eyes with your hands for about 10 seconds. While your eyes are blocked from the light, your pupils will get larger. Uncover your eyes and look at them in the mirror. You should see your pupils getting smaller and smaller as they adjust to the amount of light in the room.

Next, shine a flashlight near one eye. The sudden bright light will make your pupil get smaller. What happens to the pupil in your other eye? It should get smaller too, because the pupils work together. Like blinking, these reactions are automatic. You cannot control them.

Scientists have found that a person's pupils also get larger when they look at something interesting, and they get smaller when a person sees something upsetting. Show your friends some pictures in a magazine. Write down what happens to their pupils when they see each picture. Do their pupils get bigger when they look at a laughing baby? Do their pupils get smaller when they see a war scene?

that respond to light. These cells are named for their shapes—**rods** and **cones**. Rod cells are shaped like short, straight sticks. Cone cells look similar to upside down ice cream cones. You need both rods and cones for good vision.

The rod cells in your retina can sense tiny bits of light. They help you see shapes and movement in dim light, but the vision they provide is blurry and unclear. Cone cells are sensitive only to bright light. There are three different kinds of cone cells. Together, they allow you to see all the colors of the

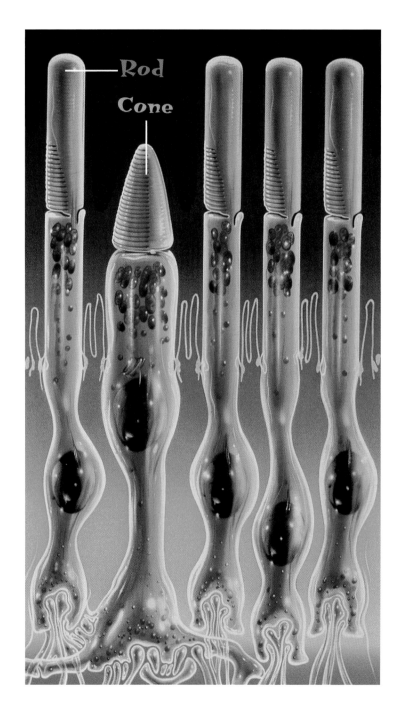

This magnified view of the retina shows four rods and one cone.

rainbow. Each cone cell reacts to just one kind of light—red, green, or blue. When you look at a green shirt, your green cone cells react, but the red and blue cells do not.

If there are just three kinds of cones, you might wonder how you see other colors. Your cone cells can work together. For example, when both your red and blue cones react, you see purple. Red, green, and blue are called **primary colors** because every other color can be made by combining them.

The three primary colors —red, green, and blue—can be combined to make many different colors.

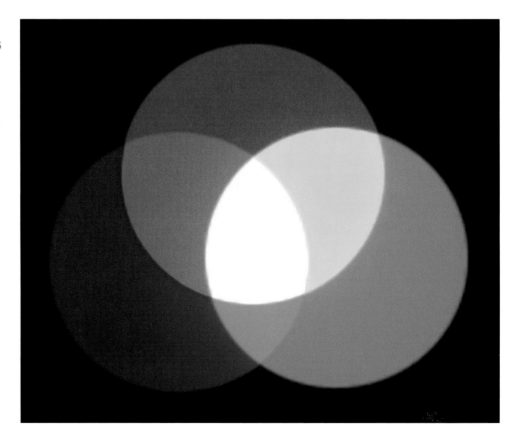

When you go outside on a moonlit evening, there is not enough light for your cone cells to work. Only the rod cells can react. That's why you can't see colors at night. Objects appear in shades of gray.

All of the cone cells are located in the **fovea**, a small area of the retina directly behind the lens. The image on the fovea is much clearer and more detailed than the image projected onto the rest of the retina, where there are only rods.

Eagle Eyes

There are about 160,000 cone cells per square millimeter in the fovea of a human eye. That may seem like a lot, but an eagle's fovea has about 1 million cone cells per square millimeter! That is why an eagle's vision is about eight times sharper than a person's. An eagle in flight has no trouble spotting a mouse scurrying through the grass far below.

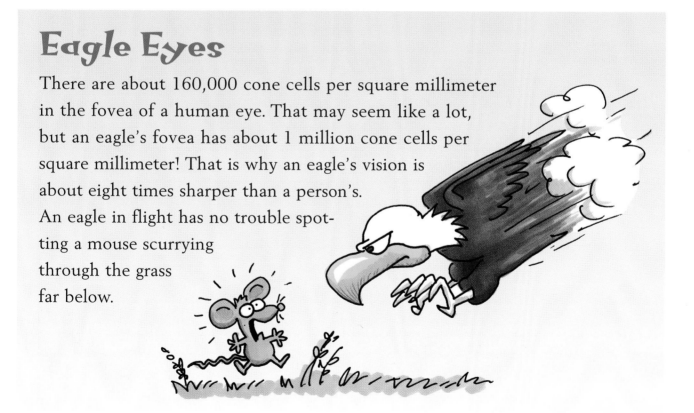

How Your Eyes See

What do you see when you read a book? You might say you are looking at a bunch of pages with words on them. What you are really seeing is light. When you look at an object, light is **reflected**—or mirrored back to your eyes.

The words you read on a page are actually reflected light.

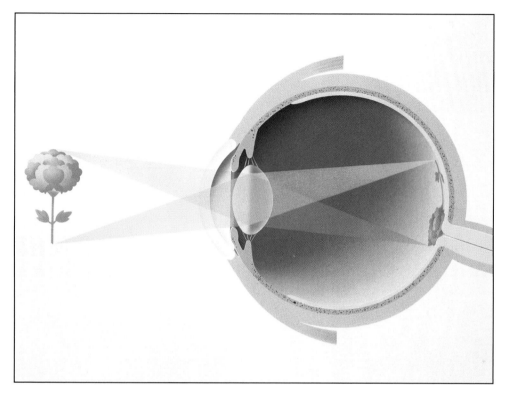

When you look at something, all the light rays from each point on the object are bent so that they fall onto a single point on the retina and form an image.

You cannot see without light. When light rays hit your eyes, they pass through the cornea. The cornea bends the light so it enters the lens. The lens bends the light rays even more.

As the light rays make their way through the liquid inside the eyeball, they continue to bend. All this bending makes the light rays from each point of the object you are looking at fall onto a single point on the retina. This process is called **focusing**. Together, all these focused points form an image—a picture of the object.

Because of the way the light rays are bent, the image that forms on the retina is upside down. This image is turned into nerve signals, which are then sent to the brain along a thick cord of nerve cells that form the **optic nerve**. Special areas of the brain receive and interpret the messages from your eyes. You don't really "see" anything until your brain makes sense out of the message from the eyes and turns the image right side up.

If you are reading a book and you hear a friend call your name, you may look up to see what is going on. When you do this, your eyes need to quickly make some changes to focus on your friend's face. To see a more distant object, muscles in your eyes will pull on your lenses to make them flatter. When you look back at the book, the muscles relax and your lenses form a more curved shape. Every time you look at something new, your eyes must refocus.

Did You Know...

A person's eyes cannot focus on nearby objects and distant ones at the same time.

Activity 2: Seeing in 3-D

Close one eye and try to walk around the room. Did you have trouble? Did you bump into anything? Walking around with one eye closed is not impossible, but it's much easier to walk when you have both eyes open. That's because seeing through just one eye gives you only part of the picture. The image looks flat and two-dimensional.

When you look at an object with both eyes open, each eye sees an image at a slightly different angle. When your brain combines these images, you get a three-dimensional view. Seeing in 3-D helps you understand how far away you are from the object. It helps you catch a ball and avoid bumping into things.

What's Wrong with this Picture?

Most of the time, we see the world in clear, colorful, three-dimensional images. But sometimes our eyes don't work properly. For some people, the pictures don't look right—they appear strange and unclear.

Sometimes your eyes need to take a rest. When you use your eyes too much for one task, the muscles may get tired and you may get blurry vision. If your eyes feel tired or achy and you have a headache, you probably have **eyestrain**. When this happens, pay attention to your eyes—take a break!

Your eyes may get tired and overworked if you use them too much.

18

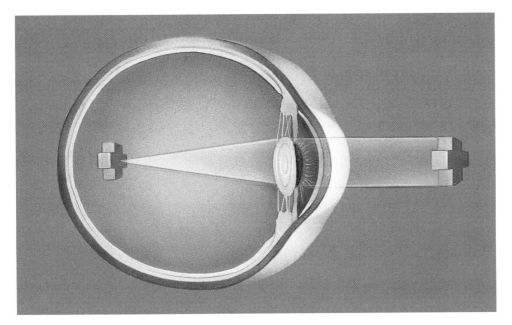

If you are nearsighted, nearby objects may look clear, but distant objects are blurry because your eyeball is so long that the light rays come together before they reach your retina.

Blurry vision may also be a sign of a more serious problem. If you can see close objects fairly well, but have trouble seeing things that are far away, you may have **myopia** (my-OH-pee-ah). Myopia is also called nearsightedness because you can only see objects that are nearby. If you are nearsighted, your eyeball is a little longer (from front to back) than normal. Light rays from distant objects meet before they reach your retina. When the light rays strike the retina, they spread out to form a blurred image.

There is no way to clear up the distant image because your lens can't adjust the focusing well enough to get the light rays to come together on the retina.

Squinting helps a bit. Fewer light rays come in through the narrowed opening, so they don't spread out as much when they reach the retina.

Nearsightedness usually shows up in young school-age kids. Nearsighted children often have trouble seeing the chalkboard clearly while sitting in the back of the classroom.

If you have no trouble seeing objects that are far away, but things that are close to you look blurry, you may have **hyperopia** (hi-purr-OH-pee-ah). Hyperopia is also called farsightedness because you can only see objects that are far away. If you are farsighted, your eyeball is a little shorter than normal. Light rays

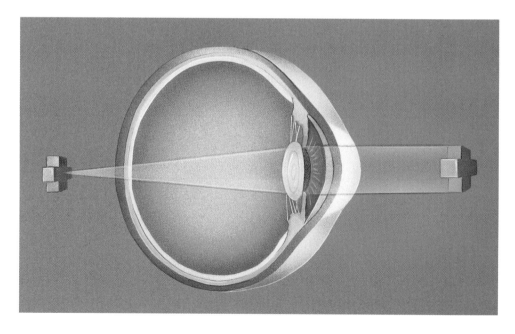

If you are far-sighted, you can see distant objects clearly, but nearby things are blurry because your eyeball is too short for the light rays to come together on your retina.

20

from close objects reach the retina before they can meet, causing a blurred image.

Normally, muscles in the eye make the lens rounder and thicker to bring close objects into focus. If you are farsighted, your muscles cannot make your lens round and thick enough to bring light rays into focus on the retina. You can see distant objects because light rays from faraway things come in nearly straight, so it is possible to focus them. However, because your eye muscles must work very hard, you may experience eyestrain and headaches.

If everything looks a little blurry to you, you may have a different condition called **astigmatism** (ah-STIG-mah-tiz-um). This means that your cornea is not shaped quite right. Your cornea is supposed to be perfectly round, like a basketball. The cornea of a person with astigmatism may be shaped more like a football. The cornea may also bulge out a little in some places or dip in at others. When this happens, light rays cannot come together at a single point on the retina.

In astigmatism, the abnormal shape of the eyes makes things both close and far away appear blurry because light rays are focused at different points on the retina.

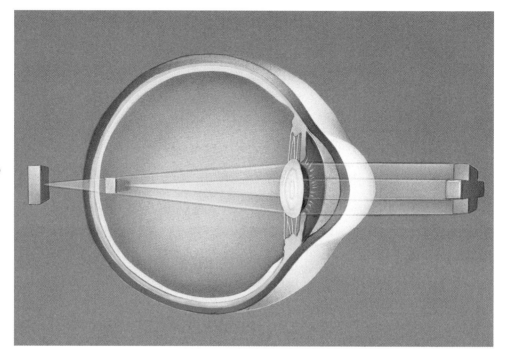

To make things even more complicated, some people with astigmatism may also be either nearsighted or farsighted. There are many different things that can affect your vision. That's why it's a good idea to have a doctor take a look at your eyes.

Some children have trouble seeing because their eyes have trouble working together. Most of the time, muscles on the outside of a person's eye turn the eyeballs inward to look at a close object. In some people, one eyeball turns too much in one direction—either toward the nose or toward the side.

As a result, each eye sees a different picture and sends a very different message to the brain. One image is clear and sharp, but the other is blurry. This may cause **double vision**—seeing two images at the same time.

Eventually, the brain may learn to "turn off" the blurry view. But using only one eye gives a flat, two-dimensional view, instead of a three-dimensional picture. This condition is known as **amblyopia** (am-blee-OH-pee-ah), or lazy eye. Lazy eye usually appears in very young children. If it is not caught early enough, the unused eye may lose its ability to see.

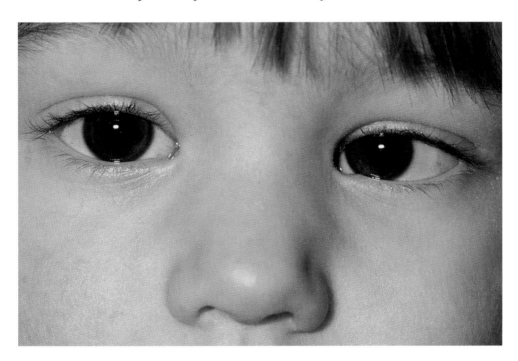

This child has lazy eye. The right eye is turning inward.

Do you have trouble telling the difference between colors? You may be **𝓬𝓸𝓵𝓸𝓻 𝓫𝓵𝓲𝓷𝓭**. Color blind people are born with missing cone cells. If you are red–green color blind, you are missing either red or green cones. As a result, red and green look like the same color. Color blindness doesn't get any worse throughout a person's life, and there is no treatment to help the condition.

Can you see the number 29? If not, you may be color blind.

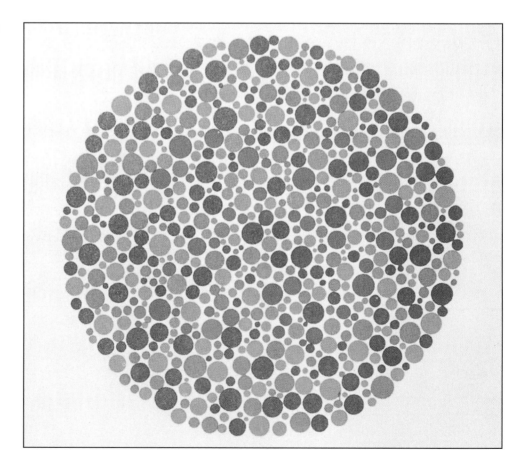

Do You Need Glasses?

How do you know if you have a vision problem? You may be so used to seeing the world in a certain way that you don't realize that anything is wrong. If things have looked blurry all your life, how could you know what clear images are supposed to look like?

Vision screening tests in schools can catch many eye problems early, but the best way to find out is to see an eye doctor. The doctor will test your eyes to make sure they are healthy and working properly.

What's the Difference?

- An ophthalmologist (aht-thuhl-MAHL-uh-jist) is a doctor who specializes in eye problems and can perform surgery.
- An optometrist (ahp-TOM-uh-trist) can treat eye problems and prescribe glasses.
- An optician (ahp-TISH-en) makes glasses and contact lenses using instructions from an ophthalmologist or optometrist.

The first thing an eye doctor will do is ask whether you've been having any eye problems. The doctor will also ask whether anyone in your family wears glasses or has any eye problems. Then the doctor will ask you to read from an eye chart. The doctor uses this eye chart to find out how well you see.

A doctor may use an eye chart to test a person's vision.

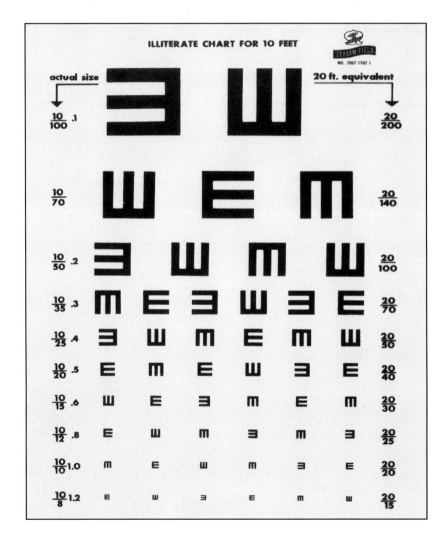

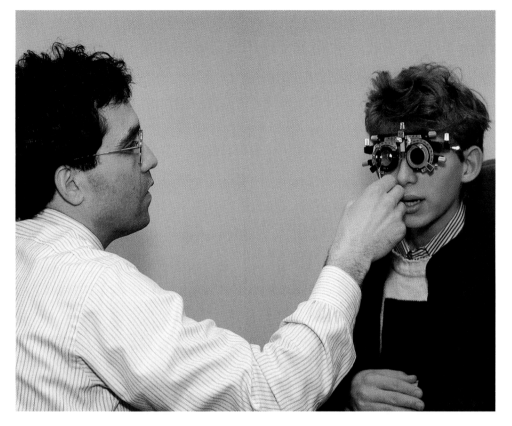

This ophthalmologist is using a machine to determine exactly what kind of eyeglass lenses will correct this child's vision.

The doctor may also do other tests to check for nearsightedness, farsightedness, and astigmatism. After studying the test results, the doctor will know whether you need eyeglasses.

The lenses in eyeglasses work like the lenses in your eyes. They are carefully made to bend light rays in a way that will make images focus properly on your retina. No two people have exactly the same eye problem, so no two people have exactly the same eyeglasses.

Nearsightedness is corrected with lenses that are thin in the middle and thick at the edges. When light rays pass through these lenses, they are bent outward just enough so that they come together at the retina.

Farsightedness is corrected with lenses that are thick in the middle and thin at the edges. When light rays pass through these lenses, they are bent inward enough to meet at the retina and form a clear image.

If you have astigmatism, light rays do not strike a single point on your retina. That can be solved with eyeglasses that add a different curve at the irregular parts of your eye. As a result, light rays bend just the right amount and focus on your retina.

Some children with lazy eye wear glasses. Others wear a patch. When their good eye is covered, they are forced to use their weak eye. Special eye exercises can also make the weak eye stronger. There is a much better chance of correcting lazy eye if it is treated early.

You may feel strange when you wear glasses for the first time. Objects may look a little blurry or unclear. This is perfectly normal. It may take several days for your brain to get used to what objects are supposed to look like.

Are Contacts for You?

Have you ever gotten an eyelash or a speck of dirt in your eye? Did it bother you so much that your eye got red and watery? If so, you might wonder how people can put contact lenses in their eyes.

Although your eyes are very sensitive to small objects, large objects that follow the curve of the eyeball don't bother them. Otherwise, the feeling of your own eyelids would drive you crazy!

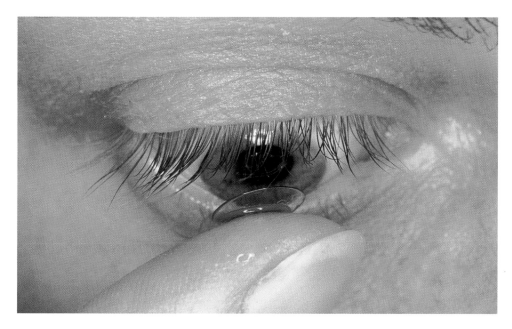

With practice, you can learn to insert a contact lens correctly.

A contact lens fits snugly over the curve of your eyeball. It floats on a thin film of tears.

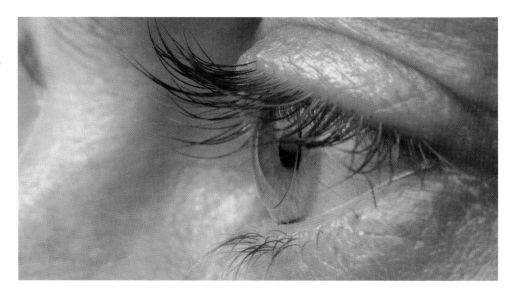

A **contact lens** is a very thin plastic disk that can be placed on the front surface of your eye. It is separated from the cornea by a thin film of tears, which holds the lens in place. Like glasses, contact lenses are designed to correct vision problems. Millions of people wear contact lenses, but they are not right for everybody.

Before you get contacts, you should ask yourself a few questions. Will you have trouble putting something in your eyes? You need to keep contacts clean and germ-free. Are you willing to spend time doing that?

People often choose to wear contacts because they think they look better without glasses. But that's not the only reason to wear contacts. They may actually be more helpful for certain eye problems, such as nearsightedness. When a nearsighted person looks through glasses, objects straight ahead appear clear but objects to the right or left may look blurry. Because contacts rest on top of the eyeball and move with the eyes, the person sees everything clearly.

Contacts come in soft and hard lenses. Soft contact lenses are very popular because they are flexible and feel more comfortable than hard contacts. They mold to the eye's shape and feel more natural, but hard lenses provide sharper vision for certain eye conditions, such as astigmatism. Soft lenses often soak up liquids, such as tears, and may pick up bacteria and particles that can irritate your eyes. There is a greater risk of the eyes becoming infected with soft lenses.

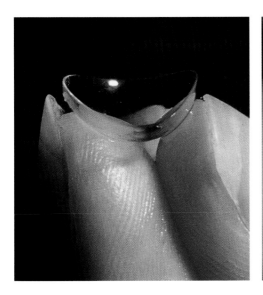 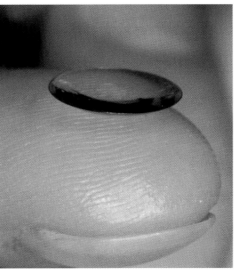

A soft contact lens (left) is flexible and can mold to the eye's curved shape. A hard contact lens (right) keeps a rigid shape–it doesn't bend.

Did You Know...

Tinted contact lenses can make your iris look like it is a different color.

Many people take out their contacts every night and clean them with a special eye-care solution. Disposable contacts—available in both hard and soft lenses—can be worn for up to 2 weeks and then thrown away. Doctors say that even disposable contacts should be cleaned every day, however.

Recently, a new kind of contact lens has become available. You wear them for 1 day and then throw them away. These lenses provide clear vision and keep the eyes healthy and free from particles—and they don't need to be cleaned.

Before you decide whether you want glasses or contact lenses, you need to talk to your eye doctor. If contacts are for you, a complete eye exam will help the doctor fit you with the right ones.

Take Care of Your Eyes

Whether or not you wear glasses, it is important to take care of your eyes. Fortunately, there are many things you can do to keep your eyes healthy and strong.

Have you ever read a book or played on the computer for a really long time? Your eyes probably started to hurt. Maybe the images even got a little fuzzy? That's because your eye muscles were being overworked.

Not even glasses can protect you from eye-strain.

Watch Out For Dry Eyes

Blinking spreads tears over your cornea, keeping it moist. If your eyes do not produce enough liquid, they may dry out and feel like they are burning. This condition, called **dry eye**, often occurs in cold weather when the air is dry. Your eyes may also dry out when they are exposed to air conditioning, smoke, wind, and even certain medications. Some people may get dry eye because they don't blink enough. For instance, people who stare at computer or TV screens blink less often than usual.

If you use your eyes for a long time, take several breaks and give them a rest. If you've been focusing on something close, stare out a window or look at a peaceful picture on the wall for a few minutes. You could also try closing your eyes and covering them with your hands for a little while. You might even want to lie down or lean back in a comfortable chair.

The glare from computer and TV screens can also make your eyes hurt. A glare causes your eyes to work harder to focus on the picture. Reducing the glare will make the picture appear clearer, so there's less work for your eyes.

Also, it's a good idea to keep at least one light on while you watch TV. In a dark room, your eyes have to strain to focus and get a clear view. Your eyes shouldn't have to work so hard.

Don't watch TV in the dark. Turning on a light can cut down the eye-tiring glare of the TV screen.

Too much sunlight can also damage your eyes. Never look directly at the sun. Most sunglasses sold today are specially designed to block out some of the sun's dangerous rays.

For a healthy body, doctors say you should eat healthy foods. Carrots, milk, cheese, eggs, broccoli, spinach, sweet potato, cantaloupe, and other foods rich in vitamin A can help keep your eyes healthy. If you look out for your eyes now, chances are you will have a much clearer, brighter future.

Did You Know...

You move your eye muscles at least 100,000 times a day.

◀ **Wearing sunglasses can protect your eyes and make you look cool at the same time.**

Glossary

amblyopia—a condition that occurs when a person's eyes do not work together properly, also called lazy eye

astigmatism—a condition in which an irregular shape of the cornea prevents clear focusing of images

color blind—being unable to tell the difference between some or all the colors that most people see

cone cells—light-sensitive cells that respond only to bright light and provide for color vision

contact lens—a plastic disk that is placed over the cornea and helps a person see

cornea—the clear covering on the surface of the eye

double vision—seeing two images at the same time

dry eye—a condition in which the eye does not produce enough tears, causing dry, hot, burning eyes

eyeball—the round, jelly-filled structure that contains all the working parts of the eye

eyelid—a movable flap of skin that protects an eye from dust and particles

eyestrain—overworked eyes that cause blurred images, tired eyes, or headaches

focusing—when all of the light rays from each point on an object are bent so that they fall onto a single point on the retina and form an image

fovea—a small area of the retina directly behind the lens. It contains all the cones and produces a clear, colorful image.

hyperopia—a condition in which distant objects appear clear, but close objects are blurry, also called farsightedness

image—the appearance of an object

iris—the colored part of the eye. It contains muscles that can change the size of the pupil to control the amount of light coming in.

lens—a clear structure behind the pupil that bends light rays to focus them on the retina

myopia—a condition in which close objects appear clear, but distant objects are blurry, also called nearsightedness

optic nerve—a thick cord of nerve cells that carries messages from the eyes to the brain

pigment—a colored chemical

primary colors—red, blue, and green, the three colors that can be used to create all other colors

pupil—the opening in the eye that allows light rays to travel to the retina

reflection—when light rays bounce from an object back to the eyes

retina—a layer of light-sensitive cells that line the back of the eyeball

rod cells—light-sensitive cells that respond to dim light, providing night vision

tear gland—a tiny structure next to the eyeball that produces tears

vision—eyesight

Learning More

Books

Anshel, Jeffrey. *Smart Medicine For Your Eyes*. Garden City Park, NY: Avery, 1999.

Ballard, Carol. *How Do Our Eyes See?* Austin, TX: Raintree Steck-Vaughn, 1998.

Collins, James. *Your Eyes . . . An Owner's Guide*. Englewood Cliffs, NJ: Prentice Hall, 1995.

Roy, Marilyn. *Eyerobics: How to Improve Your Eyesight*. London: Thorsons, 1994.

Shaughnessy, Diane. *Let's Talk About Needing Glasses*. New York: PowerKids Press, 1996.

Zinn, Walter J. and Herbert Solomon. *Complete Guide to Eyecare, Eyeglasses, & Contact Lenses*. Hollywood, FL.: Lifetime Books, 1996.

Organizations and Online Sites

Beakman & Jax

http://www.beakman.com/glasses/eyeglasses.html
This site provides information about the eye and eyeglasses, as well as other general scientific questions and answers for kids. It includes a diagram of the eye and how it works.

Common Vision Conditions

http://www.aoanet.org/common-vision-conditions.html
This site was developed by the American Optometric Association. It provides information about common vision problems and includes many tips on how to keep your eyes healthy.

National Children's Eye Care Foundation

P.O. Box 795069
Dallas, TX 75379
http://www.4woman.org/nwhic/references/mdreferrals/ncecf.htm

National Eye Research Foundation

910 Skokie Blvd., Ste. 207A
Northbrook, IL 60062
http://www.nerf.org

National Eye Institute
2020 Vision Place
Bethesda, MD 20892
http://www.nei.nih.gov/

Vision Q & A
http://www.skylog.com/eyes2020/qa.html
This site has a lot of information about vision displayed
in a question-and-answer format.

Index

Activities
  how big are your
    pupils?, 10
  seeing in 3-D, 17
Amblyopia, 23, *23*
  correction of, 28
Astigmatism, 21, 22, *22*,
    27, 31
  correction of, 28

Bacteria, 31
Blinking, 8, 10, 34
Book, 5, 14, *14*, 16, 33
Brain, 16, 23, 28

Chalkboard, 4, 5, 20
Color-blind, 24
Colors, 5, 11, 13, 24
Computer, 33, 34

Cones, 11, *11*, 12, 13, 24
  blue cone cells, 12
  green cone cells, 12
  number in eagle's
    eye, 13
  number in human
    eye, 13
  red cone cells, 12
Contact lenses, 6, 25,
    29–32, *29*, *30*, *31*
  disposable, 32
  hard, 31, *31*
  soft, 31, *31*
  tinted, 32
Cornea, 8, 9, 15, 21, 30,
    34

Darkness, 5
Double vision, 23

Dry eye
   causes of, 34
Dust, 8

Eyeball, 7, 7, 9, 19, 20,
   22, 29, 31
Eye chart, 26, *26*
Eye doctor, 6, *6*, 22, 25,
   26, 32
Eye exam, 32
Eyeglasses, 6, 25, 26, 27,
   28, 30, 31, 32, 33
Eyelids, 8, 29
Eyes
   as sense organs, 5
   caring for, 33–37
   foods for, 37
   how eyes see, 14–17
   parts of, 7–13
   resting, 18, 34
   rubbing, 5
Eyestrain, 18, 21, *33*, 35

Farsightedness, 20, 21, 27
   correction of, 27

Focusing, 15, 16, 19, 34
Fovea, 13

Headaches, 18, 21
Hyperopia, 20, *20*, 27

Image, 9, 13, 15, *15*, 16,
   17, 19, 21, 23, 27,
   28, 33
   three-dimensional, 17,
   18, 23
   two-dimensional, 17, 23
Insect, 8
Iris, 8, *9*

Lazy eye. *See* amblyopia
Lens, 8, 9, *9*, 13, 15, 16,
   19, 21, 27
Light, 8–16, *15*, 19, 20,
   21, 27, 28
Liquid, 7, 15

Mirror, 7
Muscles, 8, 16, 18, 21,
   22, 33, 37

Myopia, 19, 19

Nearsightedness, 19, 20,
    27, 28, 31
    correction of, 27
Nerve signals, 16
Night, 13

Ophthalmologist, 25, 27
Optician, 25
Optic nerve, 16
Optometrist, 25

Pigment, 8
Primary colors, 12, *12*
Pupil, 8, 9, *9*, 10

Retina, 9, *9*, 11, *11*, 13,
    15, *15*, 16, 19, 20,
    21, 27, 28
Rods, 11, *11*, 13

Scientists, 10
Shapes, 5
Squinting, 5, 20

Sunglasses, *36*, 37
Sunshine, 5, 37

Tear gland, 8
Tears, 8, 30, 31, 34
Television, 34, 35
Tests, 27

Vision, 6, 11, 18, 30, 32
Vision screening test, 25
Vitamin A, 37

About the Authors

Dr. Alvin Silverstein is a professor of biology at the College of Staten Island of the City University of New York. **Virginia B. Silverstein** is a translator of Russian scientific literature. The Silversteins first worked together on a research project at the University of Pennsylvania. Since then, they have produced 6 children and more than 160 published books for young people.

Laura Silverstein Nunn, a graduate of Kean College, has been helping with her parents' books since her high school days. She is the coauthor of more than thirty books on diseases and health, science concepts, endangered species, and pets. Laura lives with her husband Matt and their young son Cory in a rural New Jersey town not far from her childhood home.